**GARFIELD COUNTY LIBRARIES**
Rifle Branch Library
207 East Ave
Rifle, CO 81650
(970) 625-3471 – Fax (970) 625-3549
www.gcpld.org

# How Are They Made?
## Cans

Wendy Blaxland

**Marshall Cavendish**
Benchmark

New York

This edition first published in 2010 in the United States of America by
MARSHALL CAVENDISH BENCHMARK
An imprint of Marshall Cavendish Corporation

Website: www.marshallcavendish.us

This publication represents the opinions and views of the author based on Wendy Blaxland's personal experience, knowledge, and research. The information in this book serves as a general guide only. The author and publisher have used their best efforts in preparing this book and disclaim liability rising directly and indirectly from the use and application of this book.

Other Marshall Cavendish Offices:
Marshall Cavendish Ltd. 5th Floor, 32-38 Saffron Hill, London EC1N 8 FH, UK • Marshall Cavendish International (Asia) Private Limited, 1 New Industrial Road, Singapore 536196 • Marshall Cavendish International (Thailand) Co Ltd. 253 Asoke, 12th Flr, Sukhumvit 21 Road, Klongtoey Nua, Wattana, Bangkok 10110, Thailand • Marshall Cavendish (Malaysia) Sdn Bhd, Times Subang, Lot 46, Subang Hi-Tech Industrial Park, Batu Tiga, 40000 Shah Alam, Selangor Darul Ehsan, Malaysia

Marshall Cavendish is a trademark of Times Publishing Limited

All websites were available and accurate when this book was sent to press.

Library of Congress Cataloging-in-Publication Data

Blaxland, Wendy.
    Cans / Wendy Blaxland.
        p. cm. — (How are they made?)
    Includes index.
    Summary: "Discusses how cans are made"—Provided by publisher.
    ISBN 978-0-7614-4753-5
    1. Aluminum cans—Juvenile literature. 2. Tin cans—Juvenile literature. I. Title.
    TS198.C3B53 2011
673'.7228—dc22
                                                    2009039876

First published in 2010 by
MACMILLAN EDUCATION AUSTRALIA PTY LTD
15–19 Claremont Street, South Yarra 3141

Visit our website at www.macmillan.com.au or go directly to www.macmillanlibrary.com.au

Associated companies and representatives throughout the world.

Edited by Anna Fern
Text and cover design by Cristina Neri, Canary Graphic Design
Page layout by Peggy Bampton, Relish Graphic
Photo research by Jes Senbergs
Map by Damien Demaj, DEMAP; modified by Cristina Neri, Canary Graphic Design

Printed in the United States


**Acknowledgments**
The author would like to thank the following for their expert advice: Jocelyn Cory, Beverage Can Division, Amcor Australasia; Jenny Day Can Manufacturers Institute, Washington, United States, Cancentral; Silke Dittert, Public Relations, Ball Packaging, Europe; Norman Lett, UK Recycling Manager, Ball Packaging, UK; and Greg Robinson, Director, Metal Packaging Innovation, Ball Packaging, Broomfield, Colorado, United States.

The author and the publisher are grateful to the following for permission to reproduce copyright material:

Front cover photographs: Cans of paint, © Lisa Gagne/istockphoto (centre); purple can, © Feng Yu/istockphoto (bottom right); sardines in a can, Alea Image/istockphoto (middle bottom); green can, © Feng Yu/istockphoto (bottom left); yellow spray can, Soubrette/istockphoto (top left).

Photographs courtesy of:
© James L. Amos/Corbis, **9**; © Bettman/Corbis, **7** (top and bottom); © Paulo Fridman/Corbis, **14**; © Volker Moehrke/Corbis, **11**; © Neil Rabinowitz/Corbis, **25**; © John Van Hasselt/Corbis, **23** (top); © Tim Wright/Corbis, **18**; AFP/Stringer/Getty Images, **10**; Allan H. Shoemake/Taxi/Getty Images, **19**; Time and Life Pictures/Getty Images, **20**; Alea Image/iStockphoto, **3** (top), **23** (bottom); The Broker/iStockphoto, **5**; Lisa Gagne/iStockphoto, **3** (bottom), **25** (bottom); Alfed Otisi/iStockphoto, **16**; Soubrette/iStockphoto, **26** (top); Thumb/iStockphoto, **8** (right); Anu Tik/iStockphoto, **22**; Yin Yang/iStockphoto, **4**; Devon Yu/iStockphoto, **8** (left); G. P. Bowater/Alamy/Photolibrary, **17**; © Mitch Diamond/Alamy/Photolibrary, **30**; © David Levenson/Alamy/Photolibrary, **26** (top); © mediacolor's/Alamy/Photolibrary, **21**; Reuters/Picture Media/Yuriko Nakao, **29**; Reuters/Picture Media/Ilya Naymushin, **28**; Rexam Cans, **27**; Wikipedia, **24**.

While every care has been taken to trace and acknowledge copyright, the publisher tenders their apologies for any accidental infringement where copyright has proved untraceable. Where the attempt has been unsuccessful, the publisher welcomes information that would redress the situation.

1 3 5 6 4 2

# Contents

## Glossary Words

When a word is printed in **bold**, you can look up its meaning in the Glossary on page 31.

# From Raw Materials to Products

**E**verything we use is made from raw materials from Earth. These are called natural resources. People take natural resources and make them into useful products.

## Cans

Cans are airtight containers for packaging and storing goods. They are made of thin metal, opened in different ways such as cutting with a can opener or pulling a **tab**. Most cans hold food and drink.

The main raw materials used to make cans are the metals steel and aluminum. Steel is made mostly from iron, dug from the ground. Steel is used for food cans and cans for general use. Aluminum comes from bauxite, which is also mined. Aluminum is used mainly for drink cans.

Steel cans may be coated with tin to prevent rust. The inside of cans may also be painted with protective coatings to prevent the contents **reacting** with the metal cans. The outside is usually printed with ink to display product information.

*Steel cans usually contain food, and aluminum cans usually contain drinks.*

*Cans are a safe way to store many kinds of food.*

## Why Do We Need Cans?

More than half of all cans hold drinks, about one-fifth hold food, and the rest contain cosmetics, household goods, and other products. They come in a variety of designs, including large square cans, small oblong and round cans opened with keys or can openers, cans whose lids peel back, drink cans with opening tabs, and **aerosol** cans.

Containers can also be made of glass, plastic, and paper, but metal cans do not break, are strong, and last well. They provide an excellent barrier against light, gas, and moisture. Cans chill quickly, stack well, and provide the same protection year round wherever you are. They are easy to recycle and are the form of packaging most often recycled.

### Question & Answer

**What shapes do cans come in?**

Most cans are cylinders. Novelty or specialty cans, however, can come in any shape. They can be cubic, cylindrical, or even shaped like houses!

5

# The History of Cans

The first cans were made by hand and came with instructions to open them with a chisel. Using machines to make cans, however, was much faster and cheaper. Cans became so popular that by 1985, even astronauts in space enjoyed canned drinks.

## Guess What!

**During World War I, nearly two-thirds of the Allies' food came in tin cans. Governments used scarce metal to make the cans. American soldiers went into battle with a can opener hanging around their necks.**

## Cans through the Ages

**1927**
Norwegian Erik Rotheim patents the first aerosol can.

**1795**
French Emperor Napoleon offers a large prize for a way of **preserving** food for his armies.

**1846**
American Henry Evans invents a machine that makes sixty cans an hour.

**1866**
New Yorker J. Osterhoudt patents the tin can with a key opener, as found on some sardine cans.

**1938**
Soda canning begins.

1700 CE
1800
1850
1900
1930

**1810**
French sweetmaker Nicolas Appert wins the prize by inventing canning.

**1858**
American Ezra Warner **patents** the first can opener. The U.S. Army uses it during the American Civil War.

**1870**
American William Lyman patents a can opener with a rolling wheel that cuts around the rim of a can. It is still used today.

**1935**
The first canned beer is sold in the United States by the Kruger Brewing Company.

Workers solder the lids onto cans of tomatoes by hand in an early cannery in France.

**1963**
American Ernie Fraze invents the aluminum ring-pull can, after enduring a picnic without a can opener.

**1964**
The first two-piece aluminum cans are invented.

**1965**
Cans of soda appear in vending machines.

**2000s**
The development of "necked-in" cans makes it easier to stack cans in supermarkets and on shelves.

**1957** The first aluminum cans are used for beer.

**1949**
Edward Seymour, from Chicago, invents spray paint in aluminum cans.

**1967**
The first food can with an easy-opening end is made.

**1975**
The first stay-on pull-tab for aluminum cans is introduced.

1940

1950

1960

1980

2000

U.S. Army nurses during World War II prepare a canned snack over their portable stove.

# What Are Cans Made From?

**M**ost food cans are made of steel, while almost all drink cans are made of aluminum. A few cans, called composite cans, are made of paper or paperboard.

Aluminum is light, but can withstand high pressures from inside when filled with fizzy drinks.

Steel **alloy** cans are made mainly from iron, with some carbon and tiny amounts of other metals. A thin coating of tin protects the steel can from **corrosion**.

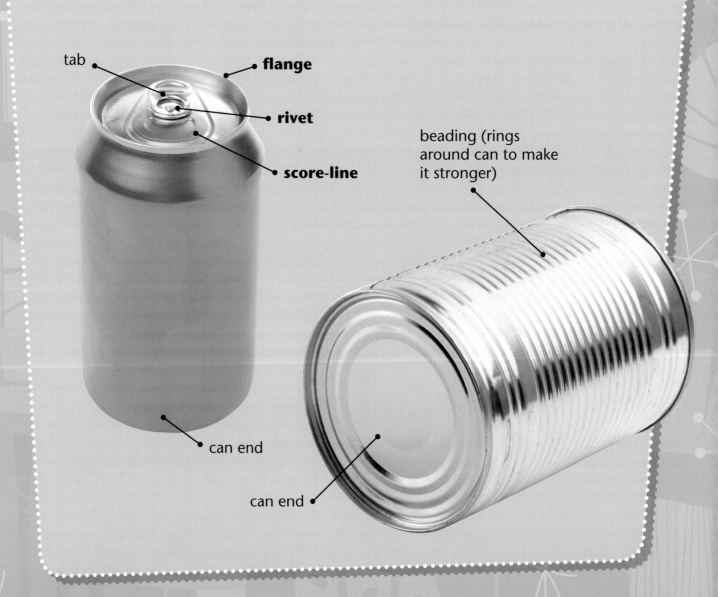

tab

**flange**

**rivet**

**score-line**

beading (rings around can to make it stronger)

can end

can end

# Materials

Many metals, protective coatings, and finishes are used to make cans. As with the making of all products, energy is also used to run the machines that help mine the **minerals**, make the metals, and shape the cans.

## Materials Used to Make Cans

| Material | Purpose and Qualities |
| --- | --- |
| Aluminum | Used in drink cans, aluminum is light, strong, easy to shape, and easily recyclable. |
| Magnesium, manganese, chromium, iron, silicon, and copper | Tiny amounts of these metals are often added to make aluminum stronger and more easily formed. |
| Steel, scrap steel | Used in food cans, steel alloy made from iron is light, easily formed, and very strong if combined with carbon. |
| Tin | Used to coat steel cans. Resists corrosion. |
| Lacquer, plastics | Lacquer protects the printing on the outside of cans. Plastics coat the inside of cans to prevent the contents reacting with the metal. |
| Paper, printing inks, varnish | Used to make decorative labels and can coatings. |

Bauxite is dug from the ground to make aluminum for cans.

# Can Design

**P**ackaging engineers work to improve how cans are designed and made, particularly by reducing their weight and making them easier to open and recycle. Usually designers make models of their new ideas. Computer-aided design helps designers work much more quickly, and therefore more cheaply. Computer programs can show the shape, color, size, and character of a product design without the need to make expensive samples.

## Saving Materials

**Manufacturers** are constantly working on ways to reduce the amount of aluminum and steel in cans. Saving materials means that cans will cost less. It also reduces the environmental impact of making cans. The latest drink cans have walls as thin as a human hair.

*Packaging engineers try to design cans that look attractive, are easy to open, and cheap to make.*

## Can Opening Designs

Manufacturers aim to design cans that are easy to open. Many food cans need a separate can opener. Some lids on food cans, such as sardines cans, can be wound around an attached opener called a key. Other cans have a top that can be peeled off right away.

Many early drink cans had problems with their methods of opening. At first, pull-tabs were used, but these caused a litter problem, and they could be swallowed if dropped into the can. Press-button cans had one button to press in and drink through and a second to let air in. However, some drinkers cut themselves, fingers became stuck inside cans and the cans could be **tampered** with. The successful stay-on pull-tab design for aluminum cans appeared in 1989. Other can-opening styles include screw tops, friction plugs for paint, and push-button tops for aerosol cans.

### Guess What!

**The color and design of a can have a big effect on how customers regard it. Manufacturers may invite top fashion designers to design the way cans look.**

*The lids on some sardine cans are peeled back with a special key.*

# From Steel and Aluminum to Cans

The process of making everyday objects such as cans from raw materials involves a number of steps. First, **ores** are mined and made into alloys. In the second stage, cans are shaped from flat sheets of metal. The cans are also printed on the outside and coated inside. In the final stage, the cans are filled, sealed, and labeled.

## Stage 1: Making Steel and Aluminum

Iron ore and bauxite are mined from the ground.

Next, the metals are separated from the ore in **furnaces**.

Iron is made into steel by adding other metals. The steel is rolled thin and coated to prevent it from rusting.

Bauxite is made into aluminum alloys and poured into **molds**. Then it is made into thin sheets.

## Stage 2: Shaping Cans

### Two-Piece Cans

First, cups are pressed from aluminum or steel sheets.

↓

Then the cans are drawn to the right length, trimmed, and washed.

↓

Next, the cans are coated inside, and the outside printed and varnished.

↓

Then the top of the can's body is reduced to the right size for the lid.

### Three-Piece Cans

First, tin-plate metal is cut into sheets.

↓

Next, the metal for the insides is coated and the outside may be printed and varnished.

↓

Then the metal is cut to size for can bodies and ends stamped out.

↓

Next, the body is rolled into a cylinder and **seamed** or **welded** shut.

## Stage 3: Finishing Cans

First, the top edge of two-part can bodies is flanged.

The bottom lid of three-part can bodies is seamed on by rolling the edges and pressing them together.

↓

Can ends are cut out.

↓

Any tabs are made separately and riveted onto the ends.

↓

Next, cans are filled.

↓

Then the top end is seamed on.

↓

Last, cans are checked and any paper labels added.

# Raw Materials for Cans

Iron and bauxite are the main raw materials used to make steel and aluminum cans.

## Iron into Steel

Rocks rich in iron are found worldwide. Iron is the world's most commonly used metal. The largest producers of iron ore, however, are Brazil and Australia. The use of iron ore grows 10 percent a year on average worldwide. China is the world's largest steel producer.

## Question & Answer

**What adds to the cost of a drink can?**

The contents of a drink can in the United States usually cost less than one cent. The can costs about seven cents, the advertising about ten. Making a narrower neck near the top saves a fraction of a cent by using less of the more expensive aluminum alloy material that is used for can ends.

*Iron ore mined from the ground is the main raw material used in making steel.*

OCEAN

Canada ✳

**NORTH AMERICA**

United States of America
✳ ★ ▮

Mexico ▮

ATLANTIC OCEAN

Jamaica ●

PACIFIC OCEAN

Brazil ❂ ● ▮

**SOUTH AMERICA**

# Bauxite into Aluminum

Bauxite, the ore from which aluminum is **extracted**, is mined in Jamaica, Brazil, Australia, and other tropical areas. Much of the aluminum used to make drink cans comes from recycled material, which reduces the need for new aluminum.

The bauxite is shipped to factories for processing, mostly in other countries. China produces almost one-fifth of the world's aluminum. Making aluminum requires huge amounts of electricity, so **smelters** tend to be situated where electric power is cheap and plentiful. Recycling makes a lot of sense, because it uses only 5 percent of the energy required to produce new aluminum.

*This map shows countries that are important to the production of cans.*

## Key

⚙ Important iron-ore–mining countries
● Important bauxite-mining countries
✳ Important aluminum-smelting countries
★ Important steel-manufacturing countries
▎ Important can-manufacturing countries

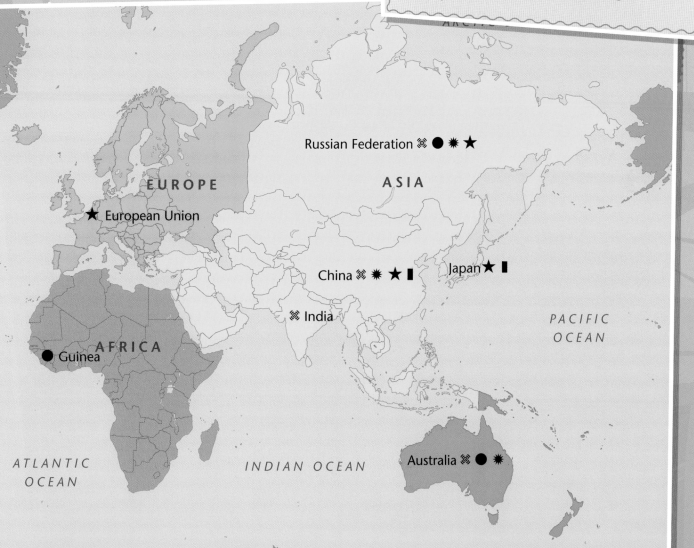

# Stage 1: Making Steel and Aluminum

## Making Steel

First, the iron ore is mined from the ground and crushed. Then the ore is smelted at high heat in huge furnaces. Smelting takes away unwanted materials and extracts the iron. Some carbon and other minerals are added to the iron to make it into steel, along with 25 percent of scrap steel. Then the **molten** steel is **cast** into slabs, which are rolled thinner and longer, first while hot, and then while cold, as thin as 0.005 inches (0.12 millimeters). After each cold rolling, the steel is heated to make it easier to work.

Then the steel is coated to prevent rust, either with pure tin or the hard metal chromium, using electricity in a process called electrolysis. Finally, the tin-plated steel is processed to stop tin oxide from forming and to make sure that later coatings will stick properly.

Red-hot molten steel is cast into slabs.

Sheets of rolled aluminum are ready to be made into cans.

## Making Aluminum

First, the bauxite ore is mined in open pits. Then it is crushed, washed, and sent to a **refinery**. There chemical reactions turn it into powdered alumina.

The alumina is then shipped to a smelter, where it is heated to high temperatures to remove oxygen. Next, recycled aluminum cans and tiny amounts of other metals are added to the molten alumina to make it stronger. Then it is poured into molds to make ingots or blocks of aluminum.

Lastly, the aluminum is cast, hammered, or rolled into thin sheets in a factory.

### Guess What!

**Aluminum begins to melt at a whopping 1220 °Fahrenheit (660 °Celsius). This means aluminum was so hard to produce before the 1850s that it was considered a semi-precious metal. The Emperor of France, Louis Napoleon, even had a special helmet and dinner service made of aluminum.**

# Stage 2: Shaping Cans

**C**ans may be made from two or three pieces.

### Making a Two-Piece Can

The aluminum or steel arrives at the factory in huge sheets. A machine punches out hundreds of cups per minute. Each cup is then forced through a series of rings to draw it out to full length. These cans have no side seams or separate bottom end. Next, they are trimmed to the right length and washed. Scrap is recycled.

The cans may be rolled against cylinders to print labels on them, and their bottoms are varnished. Next they are dried in ovens to set the printing and sprayed inside with a protective water-based coating.

The neck of the can is now created and the end is rolled over to form a flange. This will allow an end to be seamed on after filling.

## Guess What!

In the 1800s, many explorers ate food preserved in cans. Sir William Parry took a 70.5-ounce (2-kilogram) can of meat on his search for the Arctic Northwest Passage. It was finally opened more than one hundred years later. A cat happily ate the meat.

A necked-in can has a slightly wider top than the bottom, making it easier to stack.

18

Three-piece cans turn to face the right way for filling after the sides have been soldered and one end seamed on.

## Making a Three-Piece Can

First, the metal is cut into sheets. The side that will form the inner part of the can is coated to prevent the contents from reacting with the metal. Next, the side of the sheet that will be on the outside of the can may be printed and varnished.

Now the sheets are slit into flat pieces the size of individual cans, called body blanks. Can ends are stamped out of smaller sheets and packed flat into tubes to send to the manufacturer.

The body blanks are rolled into cylinders in a body-making machine. The side seam is joined by **soldering** or welding. Small wavy bends called beads are often rolled into the cylinder walls of steel cans to add strength.

# Stage 3: Finishing Cans

Finally it is time to fill and seal the cans.

## Attaching the Bottom of a Three-Piece Can

The open ends of the can bodies are rolled over on a flanging machine. One end is seamed onto the body by rolling the edges of the can end onto the flanged end of the cylinder and pressing these folds tight for a waterproof seam. The insides of cans are sprayed with a protective coating, which is baked on.

Each can is tested for leaks before being packed into cartons or onto pallets to be shipped to factories for filling.

## Making a Can End

*Workers at a soup factory check each can before it is filled.*

Blanks are cut from a sheet of special aluminum alloy to make a round shell. The shells are then coated with a sealant. Easy-opening pull tabs, if they are used, are made from a separate metal strip. A machine makes a button on the shell where the tab can be attached. Then the score, or opening area, is formed and the tab put on.

20

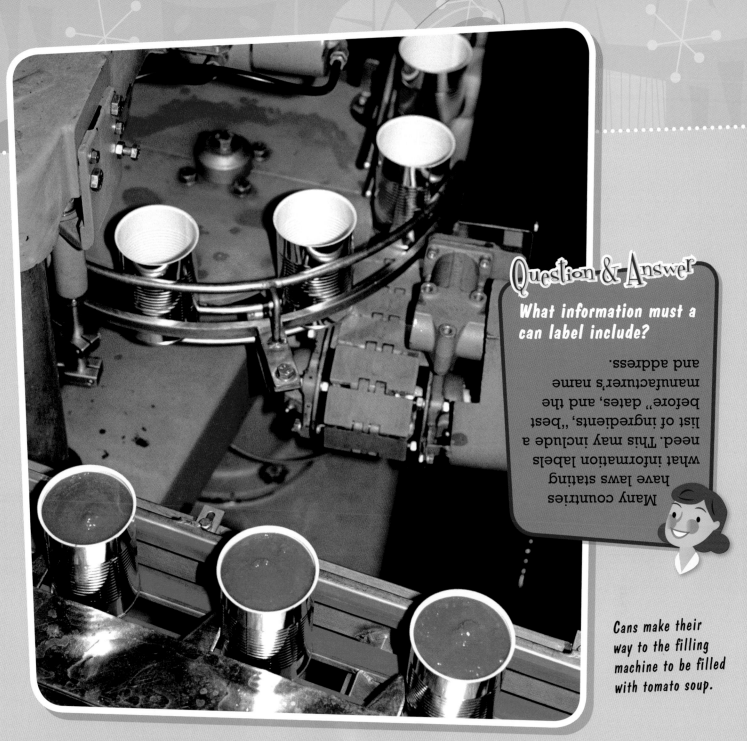

**Question & Answer**

**What information must a can label include?**

Many countries have laws stating what information labels need. This may include a list of ingredients, "best before" dates, and the manufacturer's name and address.

Cans make their way to the filling machine to be filled with tomato soup.

## Filling Cans

Drink cans are cleaned and then filled by machine. The air in the can is first taken out and replaced by gases such as **carbon dioxide**. Then the chilled drink is poured in and the can end is seamed on to seal it shut. Fizzy drinks stay bubbly because most of the carbon dioxide gas remains in the drink at low temperatures.

Most canned food is cooked inside the sealed cans at high temperatures to kill germs. The outside of the cans must be cleaned carefully after filling. They are then labeled if paper labels are used. Finally, the cans are checked to see they are filled and labeled properly.

# Packaging and Distribution

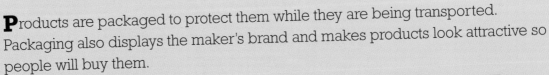

**P**roducts are packaged to protect them while they are being transported. Packaging also displays the maker's brand and makes products look attractive so people will buy them.

Machines package cans according to size and the way they will be sold. They may be put into trays to be sold singly, or into multipacks, as are many soda cans. Large paint cans will be packaged together in fewer numbers, for instance, than single-serve tuna cans.

The cans are put into cartons or shrink-wrapped in plastic and stored on pallets in warehouses. Manufacturers design the cans so that the maximum number will fit snugly on a pallet.

*Some cans are packed into cardboard cartons.*

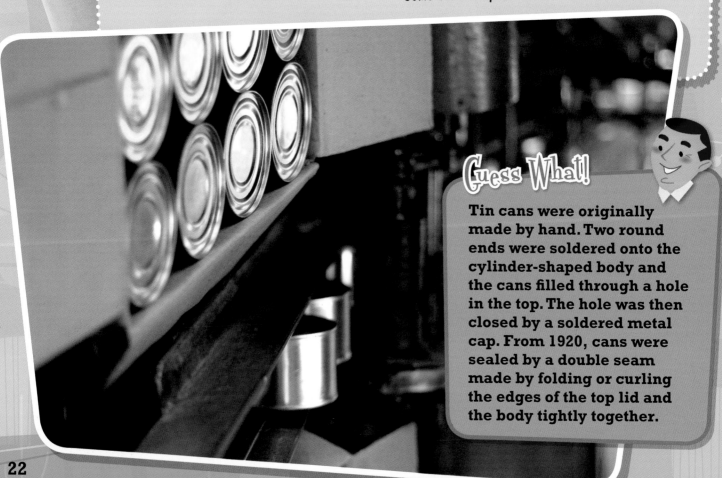

## Guess What!

**Tin cans were originally made by hand. Two round ends were soldered onto the cylinder-shaped body and the cans filled through a hole in the top. The hole was then closed by a soldered metal cap. From 1920, cans were sealed by a double seam made by folding or curling the edges of the top lid and the body tightly together.**

Drink cans are packed onto pallets and stored in a warehouse ready to be sent to retailers.

## Distribution

Empty cans are generally sent to the factories of the manufacturers who buy them to fill. They may be sold by salespeople from the canning companies at big trade fairs for the packaging industry, or over Internet sites.

Once cans are filled, they are sold along with their contents either to **distributors** or directly to **retailers**. Retailers, in turn, sell the products in cans from stores or supermarkets to individual buyers. Cans may travel long distances from where they are made to where they are filled, then to customers, often in distant countries.

# Marketing and Advertising

**M**arketing and advertising are used to promote and sell products.

## Marketing

Manufacturers promote canned food and drink as a safe, reliable, convenient, and healthy way to enjoy food when it is not freshly available. As cans improve, new features help market the product, such as having the whole lid lift off or self-heating or self-chilling cans.

The cans themselves are a very important marketing tool for their contents. Eye-catching containers with dramatic and colorful labels sway customers to choose a particular brand. When cans are sold in multipacks, the extra outside packaging, such as a cardboard case, can also advertise the product. Once customers choose a product, they are often happy to buy it in multiples, such as six-packs.

*Special design features, such as self-heating, can help sell canned goods.*

### Question & Answer

**How heavy are drink cans?**

In 1951, steel drink cans weighed 3 ounces (83 grams). Today, a steel drink can weigh 1 ounce (28 g), while an aluminum can weighs just 0.5 ounces (13 g).

The design of a new can is often advertised in attention-grabbing ways, such as these balloons in the shape of drink cans floating over San Diego, California.

## Advertising

The look of cans is very important in advertising their contents. Manufacturers of products sold in cans study what will appeal to customers and hire artists or designers to make their cans stand out. The names of products advertised on cans are also very powerful.

Cans may be used as advertising spaces for other purposes too, such as competitions or even other products. The advertisement stays in front of the consumer for as long as the original product is used. Tabs that open soda cans and even the space underneath them have recently also been used for advertising space.

There are other ways to promote canned products. Food and drink in cans are advertised in supermarket brochures and print ads, and on television and radio. So are other products in cans, such as shaving cream and furniture polish.

# Production of Cans

Products can be made in factories in huge quantities. This is called mass production. They may also be made in small quantities by hand, by skilled craftspeople.

## Mass Production

The first cans were made by hand in the 1800s. Many early cans are very beautiful or unusual. When cans were manufactured entirely by machines, however, cans were all made the same size and shape. As the contents of cans and their brands became known through advertising, people began to buy much more canned food and drink. Makers of other products, especially for the home, also saw cans as excellent packaging.

Cans are now made by automatic machines in large factories all around the world. Some machines can produce as many as 2,800 aluminum cans per minute. Big packaging companies may make bottles and cardboard packaging as well. Some cans are shipped with their contents to be sold in different countries worldwide.

*It is important to control quality on production lines in factories.*

This can, printed with glow-in-the-dark ink, is a collector's item.

**Question & Answer**

**How do you know if a food can is safe to use?**

Do not eat food from rusty, swollen, badly dented, or leaking cans.

## Unusual Cans

Cans are rarely made by hand nowadays. However, manufacturers may produce small numbers of cans in unusual designs. These include a beer can with a top that lifts off so the can becomes a cup, a square tomato soup can, self-heating cans for coffee, and even sparkly drink cans for the holidays. Cans may be printed to look wet, they can be embossed, and pull tabs can be colored or printed with logos. Other cans have inks that change color when the drink is cold enough.

Some people collect cans as a hobby. They may specialize in old cans or cans containing a particular drink. They go on expeditions to places where old cans may be found, such as former garbage dumps. Collectors trade or sell cans at swap meets or on the Internet.

# Cans and the Environment

Making any product affects the environment. It also affects the people who make the product. It is important to think about the impact of a product through its entire life cycle. This includes getting the raw materials, making the product, and disposing of it. Any problems need to be worked on so products can be made in the best ways possible.

## Mines and Metal Production

The raw materials for cans must be mined from Earth. Mining can have significant impacts on the environment. It may disturb the habitats of animals and plants and pollute the air and water with dangerous waste materials.

Metal refineries and factories use large amounts of power, especially to refine aluminum. They also cause pollution and produce gases that contribute to climate change. Dangers to workers include noise and dangerous gases in factories.

Most governments have laws to regulate the impact of mining on the environment. Companies also look for ways to reduce pollution.

*Workers in metal refineries need to wear special clothing to protect them from noise, heat, and fumes.*

A man weighs a bag packed with aluminum cans to exchange for money at an aluminum recycling factory in Japan.

## Recycling

Cans are perfect for recycling. It is much cheaper and better for the environment to recycle aluminum and steel cans than to produce them from raw materials. Metal can be recycled many times without any loss in quality.

The major expense in manufacturing drink cans is the energy needed to make the aluminum. Recycling can save up to 95 percent of this energy cost. Recycled cans may become car parts or other drink cans in as little as sixty days.

Recycling cans reduces the amount of waste in landfill and provides employment. Many countries have campaigns to encourage recycling.

### Guess What!

Because steel is magnetic, it can easily be separated from other trash and recycled.

# Questions to Think About

We need to conserve the raw materials used to produce even ordinary objects such as cans. Recycling materials such as aluminum and steel, conserving energy, and preventing pollution as much as possible means there will be enough resources in the future and a cleaner environment.

These are some questions you might like to think about:

* What is your favorite drink or food can? Why do you like it?

* What is the most exciting way you can think of to reuse cans?

* How could you improve can openers?

* What is the most unusual can you can find, either at home, at the store, or on the Internet?

* Design a can for your favorite food or drink. What qualities will it have?

* How can you recycle cans at school, at home, and in your community?

*What do you do with your empty drink cans?*

# Glossary

**aerosol**
A liquid sent out in a fine spray.

**alloy**
A material made from a mixture of metals.

**carbon dioxide**
A gas used to make drinks fizzy.

**cast**
Made into a shape by being poured into a mold.

**corrosion**
The effect of something breaking down through chemical action, like rust.

**distributors**
Sellers of large quantities of goods that have the right to sell a particular product in a certain area.

**extracted**
Removed or separated from surrounding material.

**flange**
A rim or collar to give strength and stiffness.

**furnaces**
Very hot ovens.

**manufacturers**
Makers, usually with machines in factories.

**minerals**
Substances that are mined, such as rocks containing metals.

**molten**
Heated into a liquid.

**molds**
Hollow shapes into which liquids are poured to make objects.

**ores**
Minerals or rocks containing metal.

**patents**
Has the legal right to use and sell an invention for a certain time.

**preserving**
Preparing something so that it lasts a long time or does not decay.

**reacting**
Causing a chemical change.

**refinery**
A factory where raw materials are treated to make them purer or more useful.

**retailers**
Stores that sell products to individual customers.

**rivet**
A metal stud that pins two pieces of metal together.

**score-line**
A line pressed into metal so that it can be pulled apart.

**seamed**
Joined.

**smelters**
Factories where minerals containing metals are melted to extract the metals.

**soldering**
Joining together with melted metal.

**tab**
A small flap used to open a container.

**tampered**
Interfered with to spoil.

**welded**
Joining metal pieces and filler metals using heat.

# Index